# The A to Zen of Life Maintenance

**Maya Phillips** is an accomplished trainer and Quantum Healer of 20 years' experience. Her unique spiritual viewpoint and motivating style has helped people to learn and live their dreams successfully. She has a commitment to global peace and co-operation.

**Max Comfort** advises businesses and individuals on successfully integrating their personal values in the workplace. He is actively involved in initiatives for planetary substainability, both in India with work for Tibetan refugees and in London, where he lives.

# The A to Zen of Life Maintenance

*Mapping the Emotional Mind*

Maya Phillips and Max Comfort

## ELEMENT

Shaftesbury, Dorset ● Rockport, Massachusetts
Brisbane, Queensland

Text © Max Comfort and Maya Phillips 1996

First published in Great Britain in 1996 by
Element Books Limited
Shaftesbury, Dorset SP7 8BP

Published in the USA in 1996 by
Element Books, Inc.
PO Box 830, Rockport, MA 01966

Published in Australia in 1996 by
Element Books Limited
for Jacaranda Wiley Limited
33 Park Road, Milton, Brisbane 4064

Cover illustration by Martin Shovel
Cover design by Max Fairbrother
Text illustrations by Martin Shovel
Designed and typeset by Linda Reed and Joss Nizan
Printed and bound in Great Britain by
Hartnolls Limited, Bodmin, Cornwall

British Library Cataloguing in Publication
data available

Library of Congress Cataloging in Publication
data available

ISBN 1–85230–810–9

# CONTENTS

# ACKNOWLEDGEMENTS

This book is dedicated to Michael Goldstein.

Maya would like to thank the following for their help and inspiration:

Daisy Darling for being so intransigent. The Norwich Art of Healing Group for their willingness to listen and for asking such challenging questions. Pat for her courage to heal and for her pioneer Maps. Cathie and Vikky for the hours they spent experimenting with the exercises in this book, their ever open door and most of all their understanding, love and friendship. My wonderful son, Daniel, for his patience, understanding, cheese sandwiches and cups of tea. Eve for years of practical help, love, trust, tolerance and parental devotion. Steve for telling difficult truths and being there at the end of a phone. Jo for her quiet support and diplomacy. Jazz for loving. And last, but not least, Max for sticking with the process and grounding the vision.

Max would like to thank the following for their help in preparing this book:

Jo for providing a safety net for the process of writing and for her unconditional love, encouragement and support. Delia for providing a peaceful haven for creativity. Llanarrow for its beauty and peace. Parents for teaching us so much. Maya for opening so many avenues to explore.

We would both like to thank Anthony for his introduction. Michael for his vision in publishing this book. And everyone on our editorial team at Element.

# INTRODUCTION

## Whatever Made You Buy This Book?

Don't misunderstand us, you have just bought a very special book.

We don't know what prompted you to pick it off the shelf, browse through it and then – in that sweet moment of clarity – decide to buy it. Perhaps you had a feeling about it, maybe a friend said you should get it, we don't know. Possibly you don't know either.

*How many self-help books have you read or bought over the last few years which you hoped would help you sort out your life, your blocks and your longings? And did they really work for you?*

If they did, that's great.

*Or did you perhaps find that the instructions were too complex, the task too Herculean, the book far too long and the method too complicated?*

We have found that success doesn't always come naturally because when you really want something there is often a little voice in your head shouting very loudly: 'You can't do it! You can't do it!'

*Where this book is different, is that we show you how, with a little time and effort, you can learn to recognize, to negotiate, to eliminate and to learn to co-operate with your self-doubt.*

## Why We Wrote A TO ZEN

We wrote this book because we were astonished at how effective the methods we've discovered and developed are, at how simple they can be and at how many different areas of people's lives they can touch, clarify and enrich. When you've got something that is really great, you just can't help yourself talking about it and wanting to share it with others! Okay?

We started as usual with ourselves, seeking to get answers to myriad issues that were troubling or perplexing us. We started to plot the issues on a large piece of paper in an apparently random way and then take each in turn and note our feelings about them. What we found was that the more we went into the problems on our sheet, the more insights we got.

The more we did, the deeper were the insights we gained into ourselves, other people and situations. By exploring our own personal landscapes, we became increasingly aware of the wonderful freedom that accurate self-knowledge can give if based on real honesty. We called our technique 'Emotional Mapping'.

## So What Makes Emotional Mapping So Effective?

Unlike some other methods which, although immensely useful, are largely records of an intellectual or analytical process, Emotional Mapping works with imagery inspired by the intuition, capturing and recording those fleeting moments of deep understanding too precious to be trusted to mere words, too multi-dimensional for language.

Naturally, we tried our ideas out on friends and family – as one does! The results were extraordinary and simply confirmed that the method works. Although it has already been used to help healing, it's not confined to problems. Mapping can work equally well in the classroom or the boardroom. It can be used to plan ahead, to carry out risk analysis and to manage projects. It can even be used to plan a really great holiday.

So, you can see, having found something so powerful, so useful, so exciting – we just had to tell the world!

Right now, you're the world and we're telling you. We hope you enjoy the journey.

*Developing foundation skills*

# 1

# DEVELOPING
# FOUNDATION SKILLS

This is a book about you. It is a practical exercise in self-awareness and self-recognition.

In the book, we try to avoid theory so, where you come across generalizations (when giving examples, it is quite difficult to avoid these), they are used simply to indicate direction. We are not trying to be right; what we hope to do is to assist you to develop a deeper understanding of how you tick, how you do – or don't – express your individuality and how your uniqueness can be utilized to your best advantage.

The methods in the book won't solve all your problems, nor will they make you a better person, help you win the Lottery or deliver your Prince or Princess Charming to your door. They will, however, help you choose the right frog, enjoy making a living, feel good about yourself and take on a challenge effectively.

Everything you read here has been thoroughly tried and tested, so work through the first chapters in sequence, even if you think you have used the techniques before. Naturally, there are hundreds of great books covering similar techniques. What we offer here are tools that we like, which work for us and which we believe will work for you.

We are teaching by experience, so give yourself time to do the exercises thoroughly. We will take you step by step through the process. Once you've mastered something, you won't even have to think about it – rather like breathing. You'll need a pen and notebook as you work through the exercises. We have left space in the book to give you an idea of how much room you'll need.

Chapters 1 to 9 are foundation chapters and they will give you the necessary skills and experience to use the 'A to Zen' methods effectively and to your best advantage.

After that, choose what works best for you. Dream up a destination.

Good luck and bon voyage!

Bon voyage?

Yes.

You *are* about to begin a journey.

It is almost certainly going to be an adventure during which you discover something wondrous: You.

> *His Holiness the 14th Dalai Lama once said that, now that we have explored our planet and are beginning to understand better the physical aspects of our solar system, the next great area to explore is the human mind.*

It's likely that you'll be charting your course from a point of curiosity, confusion, cynicism, expectation, desperation, frustration or some other 'ion' with, for or about something.

While you are on this journey through your mind, you can choose any method of conveyance you like: car, boat, plane, train, flying carpet, Shanks' pony, time machine or any other available contraption. But travelling can be lonely so we recommend the following companions: imagination, patience, faith, trust, integrity, laughter, forgiveness and truth. If you don't start the tour with them, you'll almost certainly meet up with them – and others – on the way.

This book will become your atlas, your compass and your A to Z. It will also be your own, personal St Bernard, bringing not brandy (sorry!) but help to get you past those treacherous crevasses of self-doubt. It will also help you to recognize where you are and to develop and follow a route or a strategy.

So, before you begin your journey:

- find out what these tools are and how to use them

- remember the safety rules

- have your pen and notebook handy

- learn to read the maps and lastly – but most importantly –

- *follow the instructions!* ◆ ◆ ◆

## INSTRUCTION

◆ Close your eyes and take three deep breaths – do that right now. Thank you!

The first lesson begins here.

## IFs

Life is full of 'ifs', 'if onlys' and 'what ifs'.

Have you noticed how often people say 'if'? It's often used as an excuse not to do something ('If it doesn't rain, I'll mow the lawn') or for not making a commitment ('If I earn enough, we'll go to Spain this summer'). It can be used to control someone's behaviour ('If you do that again, I'll smack you') or as a warning ('If you eat that cake, you'll get fat').

Here is a list of ifs we compiled during workshops, dinner dates, trips round stores and at school reunions (although there were probably some 'Thank God I didnt's' there too!).

◆ Read through our list and tick the ifs that you feel a connection with.

☐ If only I had more money I could have...

☐ If it rains we won't be able to go for a walk.

☐ If only I had a boyfriend/girlfriend, everything would be okay.

☐ What if the plane crashes?

☐ If I eat that piece of gateau I'll get fat or fatter.

☐ If only I hadn't started smoking I wouldn't be in this state.

☐ If I had a better body and face and was rich someone would love me.

☐ If I was a better lover/cook/train spotter he'd want to marry me.

☐ If I was a better lover/cook/ironer she'd want to marry me.

☐ What if he/she's seeing someone else?

☐ If it doesn't work out we can always be friends.

☐ What if his/her friends don't like me?

☐ If only he'd stop drinking so much, we'd be happy.

☐ If I'm not careful and I say something people don't like, they won't be my friends any more.

☐ What if I get made redundant and never find another job?

☐ If I don't get that job how am I going to support my family?

☐ If I take the job and mess it up I'll never get back to where I am.

☐ If I stand up to my boss I'll lose my job.

☐ If I ask a colleague for help it'll look as if I can't do my job.

◆ Now jot down some of your own here or in your notebook...

........................................................................................................

........................................................................................................

........................................................................................................

........................................................................................................

How did you do?

How many things are going on in your life that you're not happy about?

The funny thing about ifs is that they are like folds in a map. They always come at a crucial moment, just when you need to know whether to turn right or left or just keep going. They can cause feelings of fear, irritation and confusion and can undermine your confidence and your ability to see the route clearly.

As most of us are uncomfortable with uncertainty, ifs can and often do stop us in our tracks, we lose our momentum and our dreams and ambitions fall by the wayside.

Is this a familiar scenario? I bet you know someone who is always starting something but never seems to be able to finish it.

So how is it that you, our intrepid traveller, the person who started out with such enthusiasm, knowing exactly where you were going, is so easily distracted? You have probably forgotten somewhere along the path that life is not a package tour. We're not talking a mere 'seven nights and half-board' here!

Say you are going to take a holiday. You want sun, sea, sand and sex. Sounds good to us! You look through the brochure, make your choice, pay your money and get on the plane...

When you arrive at Costa del Hope it's raining, there's a two-mile oil slick on the beach and the local 'talent' has gone south to meet the US destroyer *We've Been At Sea For 6 Months And We've Got Loadsa Money To Spend*.

Your expectations, like oil-sodden seaweed, are dashed on the rocks and – like the weed – you are flattened by the weight of your disappointment. So, along with your fellow passengers from Flight BA999, you sit under a rain soaked palmtree overdosing on espresso coffee or lager and lamenting 'If only', 'If only', 'If only'!

*A man who tries to order the universe around must expect some thunderstorms!*

Life is simply unpredictable.

Here are some thoughts to help you resolve disappointment:

1  Life is a teacher – it is full of opportunities disguised as problems.

2  Resistance to learning is futile – you learn something new every day (even if you don't notice) just by reading a newspaper or watching *Baywatch*. Yes, really!

3  Choosing your assignments (opportunities) is much more fun than doing detention (having something forced on you).

4  You get to choose your assignments when you take time to recognize that part of your life isn't working as well as it should be or that you're unhappy about something.

5  There is a skill to discovering how, why, what, when and where you are not happy. It's called:

## Self-Assessment

The three most important skills you need to assess a situation or yourself are:

1  Recognition that there is a problem

2  Honesty (with yourself and others)

3  To be in the present – ie not longing for the past, not worrying about the future but facing up to what needs attention right now.

Why?

Because it's vital to know where you are, either literally or metaphorically, as it's almost impossible to get 'there' without knowing where 'here' is. Christopher Columbus would agree; he thought he was heading for India and ended up in the Caribbean. The poor fellow died never knowing that he'd discovered a new continent. Life, as they say, is a beach.

## INSTRUCTION

◆ Stop reading.

◆ Close your eyes and take three deep breaths.

◆ Do it right now.

◆ Open your eyes and carry on.

Self-assessment is not as scary as it sounds but it is harder then you think. Here's why:

Cast your mind back to the festive season – Christmas, Hanukah, Solstice – whatever you celebrate it as.

Traditionally it's a time of love, joy and 'peace to all men'. It's also a time of *shopping!*

There you are on the pavement, staring in through the windows at Macy's or Harrods, desperately seeking inspiration in the elaborate, red- and green-tinselled interiors. The image they convey is comforting, full of warmth, wealth, style and satisfaction; carefully cluttered, colourful perfection. Evocative, isn't it?

What you are looking at is a shop window display, an advertisement. It is someone's 'idea' of Christmas, designed to make you feel good, go inside and spend lots of money.

Think about it for a moment. Does your Christmas look or feel like that?

It is a fantasy and it's the Christmas fantasy that we all, to one degree or another, strive to create – or avoid! We make it the measure of:

• how much we are loved

• how much we love our family and friends

• how many friends we have

- how generous, unselfish, thoughtful we are
- whether we are good, worthwhile people
- how mean other people can be
- what extraordinarily bad taste some family and friends have!

So you can see that often a fantasy is far more seductive than reality and that's why *being in the here and now* is a skill that needs to be worked at.

Of course, both fantasy and reality are true. Fantasy is true when you believe in it and act 'as if' it's true. Reality is true when you remove the emotion, take off those rose-tinted glasses, and get objective.

Don't get us wrong. We're not knocking fantasy. There is great value and delight in imagination but it can be like chocolate gâteau: it's irresistible on the dessert trolley but once you get stuck in, you find that all the yummy bits are on the top of a slab of ordinary sponge. Okay, so we're not going to the right restaurants! But we hope you get the point.

In the next chapter we'll be talking more about Reality and 'Reality'. And food!

*Reality and 'reality'*

# 2

# REALITY AND 'REALITY'

*Often people attempt to live their lives backwards;*
*they try to have more things, or more money,*
*in order to do more of what they want,*
*so they will be happier.*

*The way it actually works is the reverse.*
*You must first be who you really are,*
*then do what you need to do,*
*in order to have what you want.*

MARGARET YOUNG

From our experience, developing a healthy relationship with Reality takes a little time, then lots of practice.

In the last chapter, we talked of that Christmas store window. Let's get rid of the window dressing, throw away the tinsel, undress the dummies, turn off the bright spotlights and see what we are left with in the cold, wintry daylight.

In order to help you out here are some examples:

1  An overweight woman tells everyone that she really doesn't eat much but her friends see that she eats heartily.

2  You paid a vital cheque into your account but you didn't allow enough time for it to clear and the bank charged you for an

overdraft. Although you clearly screwed up, you told yourself: 'It wasn't *my* fault', or you bitched about the bank.

3 'He loves me really; I know because he tells me he does,' says a woman with a black eye.

4 'I can stop whenever I want; I just don't want to yet,' says a 40-a-day smoker.

5 'I own my home,' says the man with the 100 per cent mortgage.

6 A man walks down the street. He has had his home repossessed by the bailiffs that morning and his wife has run off with the milkman. A friend greets him: 'How are you?' 'Fine, yeah, great!' he says.

7 'Yea, though I walk through the valley of the shadow of death, I will fear no evil.' (Psalm 23) That's all well and fine but the guy who wrote it didn't live on the Lower East Side.

> *Prayer indeed is good, but while calling on the gods a man should himself lend a hand.*
> HIPPOCRATES

Now it's your turn to think of situations where people totally convince themselves about something and in the process lie to themselves, deny their real emotions or avoid the painfully obvious.

◆ Put your thoughts down here or in your notebook...

........................................................

........................................................

........................................................

........................................................

........................................................

Now that you've done that...

◆ close your eyes

◆ take three deep breaths

◆ be as honest as you can: consider where you might convince yourself about something that is not necessarily true. You could ask a friend to confirm your self-perceptions.

◆ Please write down your thoughts.

........................................................................................................

........................................................................................................

........................................................................................................

........................................................................................................

........................................................................................................

Okay. How much window dressing did you need to remove?

Well done; now that you can do this, your Honesty is beginning to take care of itself. Add to that the fact that you completed your list of ifs in chapter 1 and you are beginning to recognize a problem when you see it, so...

◆ pat yourself on the back and remember: these skills get easier with practice.

We bet you didn't know you could learn so much in a few minutes.

Okay. Time for a break, so...

◆ put the book down,

◆ go for a walk and come back to us later.

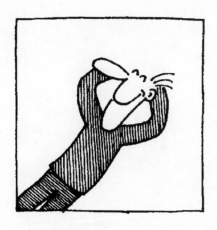

*Relaxing*

# 3

# RELAXING

*A man who holds his breath too long, suffocates.*

Now you've looked at the ways we all kid ourselves, your sense of Reality will be starting to take shape! The next thing you need to learn in order to get the best out of this book is to relax.

You can spend a great deal of time and money training to relax, having wonderful fun in flotation tanks, submerged up to your chin in healing mud or learning to tie your ankles in a bow behind your neck. We'd like to teach you the fundamentals – now! Here! If you're a total novice you'll need to do this chapter; if you've 'done' relaxation, you can skip it if you like – but you might enjoy it anyway!

First things first: start slowly, read the instructions, then – and only then – do the exercise.

The following cartoon shows what you do. Think of something wonderful...

◆ Do this for 5 minutes – start now, before you read any further.

OK, so what happened?

- Did the phone ring?
- Did you pick it up?
- If you didn't, did you worry about who it was?
- Did you think about what you were going to have for dinner tonight?
- Did you get an itch?
- Did you get fidgety?
- Did you feel silly, wired, or think 'What the hell am I doing this for'?
- Did you daydream?
- Did you fall asleep?
- Other?

Don't worry – whatever you experienced is fine.

This is what we experienced when *we* were first learning to relax:

- Aches and pains
- Tension in back and neck
- Cold feet
- Feeling really silly (particularly in a group)
- Feeling guilty about wasting time
- Pins and needles
- Sore and numb bum
- Nagging inner voices
- Irritation with outside noises
- Intrusive un-wonderful thoughts
- Wondering what the hell we were doing this for anyway
- The dog would bark, the phone would ring, or the smoke alarm reminded us that we had left toast under the grill
- An overwhelming desire for strong coffee

Whatever happened the first time, try it again doing it this way.

**EXERCISE**

- Get comfortable in a chair or on the floor cross-legged or leaning against something. (Please don't lie down as we don't want you falling asleep!)
- Think of something wonderful.
- You can stare into space or close your eyes.
- Every time you realize you're thinking about feeding the dog, the unpaid electricity bill or the fact that your new partner's six children are coming to stay, think of something wonderful.
- Try this for five minutes.

> If you get aches and pains or feel unusually hot or cold don't worry. It's because tension is leaving your body. Soon you will begin to feel more relaxed.

Well, what happened?

- Write down your experiences here or in in your notebook...

......................................................................................................

......................................................................................................

......................................................................................................

......................................................................................................

......................................................................................................

If you couldn't *remember* anything wonderful, think of something you would like to experience – make it fun, use your imagination, yes – go on, throw caution aside – fantasize!

We would expect that every time you thought of something wonderful...

- Your body relaxed
- Your hearing sharpened
- Your breathing slowed down
- You might have felt tired

◆ If you don't think you felt any of the above just keep thinking of something wonderful.

◆ Keep thinking of something wonderful.

◆ Keep thinking about something wonderful until your body feels relaxed.

These are some of the things we feel when we relax:

- Twitching or ticking muscles
- Our body feels lighter
- Our body feels heavier
- Sometimes hands, feet or face can start tingling or go numb
- Our breathing can get very deep or very shallow
- Sometimes we can feel very chilly, so it may be good to have a blanket handy

- Our stomach may rumble
- We can hear our breathing
- Our eyelids can feel heavy, or they might even feel as if they are stuck together
- Our eyelids flicker uncontrollably
- We become very aware of external sounds, but they don't bother us
- Sometimes we experience a sense of pleasant expectation
- Waves of energy move through us

Feeling more reassured?

Okay?

As practice makes perfect...

◆ Try again please

◆ Record your experiences...

........................................................................................................

........................................................................................................

........................................................................................................

........................................................................................................

........................................................................................................

Before we move on, a further word or two about relaxation. Medical practitioners all agree that it's good for your body, it reduces the effects of stress, it's a mild but natural tranquillizer, it increases blood supply to muscles and organs and, when practised regularly, it helps make you feel much better about yourself, life and the universe.

We have a lot more we could say about relaxation, but – for the moment – consider this:

**Relaxation frees up energy.**

Try this exercise now:

◆ Clench your fist hard, make it really tight.

◆ Tighter!

- Keep your fist clenched tight while you continue reading this page...
- Notice whether your arm tenses up too.

Is your hand aching?

Okay. Count to 30 – slowly!

- Release your clench now.

Does your hand start to tingle?

What about your arm – has all the tension gone?

- Shake it a little.

Does that help?

Releasing your fist freed the energy being held there; now you can use it for doing something else.

When you relax, you give your whole body the opportunity to free up and divert all that pent-up energy into something more productive or enjoyable – and that includes good, quality sleep!

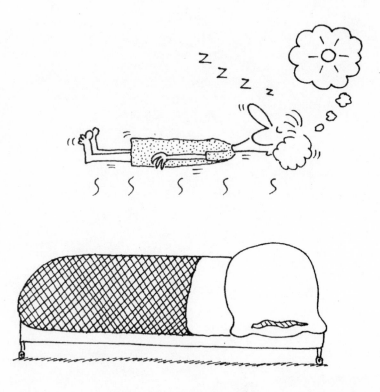

*Connecting body and mind*

# 4

# CONNECTING BODY
# AND MIND

*If the body is ignored by the mind,*
*it has to make a lot of noise to be noticed.*

*To have the perfect body,*
*create the perfect mind.*

Have you noticed that when you think good, you feel good?

The same is true in reverse. When you feel good, you think good.

So it would be reasonable to deduce that the way you think has a direct effect not just on your mood, but on how you physically feel. Not only that...

Could your body actually tell you how you are 'really' feeling? In some situations, your body can be more honest with you than your mind. Let's look at this concept more carefully.

Can you remember a time, on vacation perhaps, when you were lying on a beach, feeling good, listening to the surf, feeling the sun's rays warming your skin and breathing in that fresh, invigorating sea air? It felt good and your mind was a million miles away from the city, the office, the garbage you forgot to put out and your pending final exams.

In a situation like this you can get so relaxed, so physically comfortable that it's almost difficult to think at all. You become immersed in the feeling; your mind and your emotions become calm. You are in a truly relaxed, mellow mood, daydreaming and unaware of your thoughts.

Your mood is an indication that you've unwound; the lethargy in your body also indicates that your mind has stopped thinking actively and that you are automatically – and without being aware of it – letting tension be released.

◆ Go on – think about it now.

Feels good doesn't it? Your mind, body and emotions have had a direct effect on each other and the result in this case is positive deep rest, relaxation, release and rejuvenation!

Right now you are going to utilize this natural phenomenon and develop your ability to link your body to your feelings – this is called 'tuning in'. It's a bit like tuning in to a radio or TV station.

You are going to 'tune in' to yourself, as opposed to 'tuning out' by worrying or thinking about other people and what they are thinking or doing. This skill is important, because when you are Mapping, you are the most significant person in the process. It is your journey and it is what you discover and how you respond to it that will make the difference in your life.

Incidentally...

Worrying about what others are thinking, doing or about to do is a complete waste of time because you cannot know precisely what is going on in someone else's head. Even they probably don't know half the time!

Try *asking* them instead – it's far less hassle and it frees up energy. You can then be productive, be in the present and make yet another difference in your life!

So, here we go. Please follow the instructions carefully, as before.

**EXERCISE**

◆ Close your eyes, take three deep breaths, open your eyes and then do the following exercise...

Please remember to read through the whole exercise first.

◆ Get comfy.
◆ Be still.
◆ Relax.
◆ Close your eyes.
◆ Start by giving attention to your left hand. (If you find this difficult, see a picture of it in your mind.)
◆ Make a mental note of what happens to that hand as you pay attention to it. And what happens to the rest of your body while you focus on that hand.
◆ After a few seconds, take a deep breath and open your eyes.
◆ Try it now.
◆ Take a deep breath.
◆ Make a note of what happened.

..................................................................................................

..................................................................................................

.................................................................................................

.................................................................................................

.................................................................................................

This is what we would expect to have happened:

- You will have become much more aware of your left hand.
- It may feel lighter, heavier, tingly, etc.
- The rest of your body 'disappears'.
- The rest of your body automatically relaxes.

If nothing happened, don't worry, relax, think of something wonderful for a minute or two and then try again. If – and only if – this exercise is impossible for you, think about someone holding or stroking your hand.

Okay. Let's try that again.

◆ But this time focus on the left hand for about 30 seconds and then shift your focus to your left foot.

◆ Do that now, then take a deep breath and write down here or in your notebook what happened.

.................................................................................................

.................................................................................................

.................................................................................................

.................................................................................................

.................................................................................................

Now that you've learnt to do that, we're going to practise with the rest of your body.

◆ Relax, think of something wonderful.

◆ Now focus on your right foot.

◆ Make a mental note of what happens to the foot as you pay attention to it. What happens to the rest of your body while you focus on your foot?

◆ Try it now.

This is what we would expect to have happened:

- Your foot begins to tingle or to get warmer/colder.
- Some parts of the foot may become more noticeable, for example your big toe.
- You become less aware of the rest of your body.
- Your body feels light but your foot is solid on the ground.
- You may have discomfort somewhere else.

Okay. Let's try that again but this time...

- Focus on the right foot for about 30 seconds and then shift your focus to your left arm.
- Do that now, take a deep breath afterwards and then write down here or in your notebook what happened.

.........................................................................................................................

.........................................................................................................................

.........................................................................................................................

.........................................................................................................................

Now we'll focus on your left arm.

- Make a mental note of what happens to the arm as you pay attention to it. And what happens to the rest of your body while you focus on that arm?
- Try it now.

This is what we would expect to have happened:

- Part of your arm may tingle.
- You may become aware of muscle tension in your shoulder.
- You may become aware of an aching in your arm.
- You may become aware that the rest of your body feels 'fuzzy' compared to your arm which feels 'sharp'.

Okay. Let's try that again but this time...

- Focus on the left arm for about 30 seconds and then shift your focus to your right leg.

◆ Take a deep breath at the end of the exercise.

◆ Do that now and then write down what happened.

..............................................................................................................

..............................................................................................................

..............................................................................................................

..............................................................................................................

Now you're getting the hang of this, try it with the torso itself. What happens to the torso – the hips, the stomach, the chest, the shoulders? Move your attention around, check them all out. What happens to all the other parts while you're focusing on the torso?

◆ Try it now.

This is what we would expect to have happened:

• You become aware of muscle tension in your back.

• Your stomach may feel quite full.

• You become aware that your gut is very relaxed.

• You may find that tension is released as you become aware of it and put your attention into it – this is because you are learning already and it's becoming automatic.

• You may find your attention wandering.

• You may get irritated.

Okay. Let's do it one more time but now...

◆ Focus on a part of your torso for 30 seconds and then shift your focus to an internal organ, like your heart, liver, or kidneys.

◆ Do that now and then write down here or in your notebook what happened.

..............................................................................................................

..............................................................................................................

..............................................................................................................

..............................................................................................................

As you become more adept at this you can focus on other body parts and internal organs. This is a great way of releasing deep tension but, as we are going to look at that in the next chapter, don't worry about it for the time being.

For those of you who are having difficulty in either doing or maintaining the exercises in this chapter, here is an exercise that helps even the most intransigent stress-heads! Get someone to read this to you very slowly or, if that's difficult, record it yourself remembering to leave the [pauses] where we've indicated them.

◆ Take a deep breath.

[Pause for a really deep breath]

◆ Think of something wonderful.

[Pause for 15 seconds]

◆ Keep thinking something wonderful until you feel relaxed.

[Pause for 20 seconds]

◆ Now begin to wonder how much more relaxed you could be and, as you wonder, be aware of your right hand.

[Pause for 15 seconds]

◆ Allow your right hand to be the most important thing in your mind. If you can, see an image of it in your mind.

[Pause for 15 seconds]

◆ Remember, thoughts are like water; they flow randomly and create their own momentum. Imagine your hand is in running water; feel the water moving through your fingers.

[Pause for 5 seconds]

◆ Now see the water moving down your body and into your feet.

[Pause for 10 seconds]

◆ When your feet are full of water, feel it trickling between your toes.

[Pause for 10 seconds]

◆ Make the water very warm and, after a minute, imagine it to be ice cold.

[Pause for 60 seconds]

◆ Feel the different sensations. How are they?

[Pause for 20 seconds]

◆ Allow the water to run away into the ground, deep underground.

[Pause for 10 seconds]

◆ Slowly open your eyes.

Great. From now on, notice how, every time you are asked to change your attention from one part of your body to another, you can allow your attention to flow, like water. Practise this exercise as often as you can. It need only take 5 minutes of your time and will help you develop the ability to focus rapidly and thoroughly.

*Letting go...*

# 5

# LETTING GO…

*A sponge held in a clenched fist lets no water in.*

Now that you have...

☺ Learnt about Reality

☺ Learnt to relax

☺ Learnt to focus attention on your body...

... the next step is a brief but important lesson in releasing tension or pain from your body. You have already learnt the basics so you will find this very easy.

As you do not want to be interrupted while you're doing these exercises, take a few moments to prepare your space. Take the phone off the hook, check your diary to make sure there's no chance of being descended upon by friends. See to the cat or the dog or the canary and make yourself a cosy, nurturing space to work in.

This is what you are going to do, so...

Read the instructions first, then practise.

◆ Get comfy.

◆ Relax.

◆ Close your eyes.

◆ Focus on your body.

◆ Start at your feet and briefly (5–10 seconds) pay attention to your calves, thighs, pelvis, abdomen, lower back, chest, upper back and shoulders, upper arms, lower arms, hands, neck, head and face.

◆ Make a mental note of any areas of discomfort.

◆ Think of something wonderful.

◆ Breathe in and, as you do so, imagine that you are breathing sunlight into all the parts of your body that are tense. Allow yourself to *feel* or simply *imagine* that the warm sunlight is dissipating the tension.

◆ As you breathe out imagine that you are releasing the tension from your body with your out-breath.

◆ Continue breathing the light in for about 5 minutes.

◆ Then simply sit quietly, focusing your attention on your feet, and breathe normally for about a minute.

◆ Open your eyes.

◆ Write down your experiences here or in your notebook...

.......................................................................................................

.......................................................................................................

.......................................................................................................

.......................................................................................................

.......................................................................................................

.......................................................................................................

.......................................................................................................

This is what we would have expected you to notice:

☺ I got more relaxed.

☹ I got restless.

☺ Once I focused on my body it was easy to find tension.

☹ The pain increased slightly when I started to breathe in the sunlight.

☺ After a few minutes the pain abated.

☺ I almost fell asleep.

☺ I felt more relaxed after the exercise than I did before.

This last exercise will help you to deal with the inevitable physiological and emotional effects of problem solving. So try to practise it once or twice a day on a regular basis. It acts as a spring clean, clearing away the cobwebs in your mind and body.

It will also act like the safety valve on a pressure cooker – you! – by helping you let off steam gently and safely.

That's all; easy, wasn't it? So please put the book down, go for a walk, hang out the washing or do some digging – get physical!

At this point it's probably important to say that you don't *have* to get physical, make coffee, hang out the washing or walk the dog at the end of every chapter, although we're sure the dog wouldn't complain!

But do allow yourself time for integration, rather than rushing through the book to find answers.

*You won't find answers in this book. Because you are currently engaged in creating them.*

*Visualization*

# 6

# VISUALIZATION

*Albert Einstein says 'Imagination is more important than knowledge.'*

*We say 'If you have the flair to see your future, you are no longer taking footsteps in the dark.'*

You have now learnt how to recognize a problem, to relax, to focus on your body and to release some of that tension.

The next important skill to learn is visualization; that is allowing or instructing your imagination to develop pictures in your mind. Sometimes these pictures will be from memory and sometimes you will create them out of nowhere.

Just for fun, try this exercise. Read it through first please!

**EXERCISE:**

◆ Get comfy.

◆ Close your eyes.

◆ Think of a triangle (or try not to think of one because if you think too hard it won't work. Remember Luke Skywalker in '*Star Wars*' learning about the Force?).

◆ What colour is it?

◆ What colour is the *background*.

◆ Open your eyes.

With your eyes open, can you remember your triangle?

What happened?

◆ Write down your results...

........................................................................................................

........................................................................................................

Everyone 'sees' differently. If you ask a friend to do the exercise above and then ask what he or she saw, you would discover that you were not thinking about the same triangle at all.

Let's do this again.

◆ Right now, while you are reading this page, think of a tree.

How tall is it, what season is it in, does it bear fruit?

These are the trees Maya saw in her mind as she read this page:

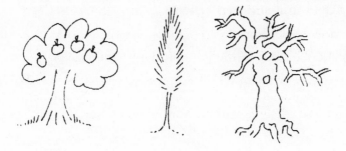

And these are Max's:

Do they look anything like yours?

For the moment, what and how you 'see' inside your head is unimportant. It's simply the process of inner 'seeing' and your recognition that you can and *do* 'see' that will help you to develop this skill.

Often, when you become conscious of your inner sight, you will just have an awareness of an image. At other times you will see things in glorious Metro-Goldwyn-Meyer Technicolor. Sometimes you will need to close your eyes to enhance an image and then again you may merely stare into space to conjure up a daydream.

Remember, whether you realize it or not, you 'see' all the time, in fact every time you think.

Here's another exercise.

Remember to read it through before you start.

◆ Get comfy.

◆ Relax.

◆ See a triangle as before.

◆ Change it to a pyramid.

◆ Make a door in it and step inside.

◆ Try to 'see' what colour it is.

◆ Now make the floor of the pyramid into a trampoline.

◆ Bounce up and down on the trampoline.

How does it feel?

◆ Write down here or in your notebook what happened in your pyramid.

.........................................................................................................

.........................................................................................................

.........................................................................................................

.........................................................................................................

You have now learnt the basic skill of creative visualization. It was easy, wasn't it?

Okay. Now close your eyes, take three deep breaths, put the book down and come back to it later.

*It's as natural to daydream and to use your imagination as it is to breathe.*

*Tuning in to emotions and feelings*

# 7

# TUNING IN TO EMOTIONS AND FEELINGS

Feelings and emotions are not the same thing.

Confused? Then ponder on this:

> *When traversing life's map feelings act as a compass – they indicate the direction which will lead us to where we want to be.*

Emotions demonstrate how you experience events that happen in the big wide world. They are like a barometer, up when the day is fine, and down when you are under pressure. In other words thay are responses to life. As a compass they can be pretty untrustworthy as they can get you into a state of fear, distraction or exhilaration and can also lead you into a quandary, up the garden path or round in circles.

Feelings on the other hand are about insight, instinct, gut responses and inner knowing. They are a sense of something comfortable or right. We usually lost touch with these impressions in childhood when we learnt that big or bigger people's needs came first. Then in order to please others, get brownie points and avoid being shouted at we hid our hopes and our tears and learnt about fear and resentment instead.

However you lost your ability to respond to your feelings (bossy sister, overbearing father or the desire for an extra portion of ice-cream), the exercises in this chapter will help you to remember what it feels like to know exactly what you want. How you then get it is up to you.

Okay. Let's try something. You now know how to relax and focus on your body. The next step is learning to combine the two.

Here goes. Read the instructions first, then try them out.

**EXERCISE**

◆ Get comfy.

◆ Relax.

◆ Close your eyes.

◆ Focus on your body.

◆ Think of something wonderful!

◆ Recognize how 'wonderful' feels and where in your body this particular 'wonderful' lives.

◆ Then name it – ie Lust, Love, Excitement, Happiness and so on.

Isn't it amazing to find out how many different kinds of good feelings you can have and where you feel them?

Just to make sure you've got the hang of it...

◆ Do it again using a different kind of 'wonderful'.

◆ Try this exercise with three or four different feelings and memories.

Later on, when you have learnt more about Mapping you can use this exercise to connect with deep feelings and negative habitual behaviour (in order to break it!).

Okay. Now let's look at something a bit more challenging.

Let's try working with a less comfortable feeling like Anger, Upset, Frustration.

> NOTE! Work with a feeling or memory that isn't too disturbing.
>
> DON'T try to run before you can walk: you are learning a sequential technique and you are only on Foundation Level at present.

Read this exercise through first:

**EXERCISE**

- ◆ Get comfy.
- ◆ Relax.
- ◆ Close your eyes.
- ◆ Focus on your body.
- ◆ Think of something frustrating, painful or sad (we'll call it yukky – that covers most things!).
- ◆ Recognize how 'yukky' feels and where in your body this particular 'yukky' lives.
- ◆ Then name it – ie Hurt, Rejection, Anger, Pain, Sadness and so on.
- ◆ Then relax and think of something really wonderful until you feel calm and comfortable again.
- ◆ When you're ready, open your eyes.

Clearly, thoughts create sensations (emotions and feelings) in your body and vice versa. We all know that emotions rise rapidly in situations of excitement, like the last few moments of the World Cup. And we can relate to the gut-wrenching feeling of saying goodbye to someone we love. What we hope that you will rediscover through these exercises are the less dramatic quieter feelings that lie under the surface.

*When I ask a question, how do I feel?*

# 8

# WHEN I ASK
# A QUESTION, HOW DO
# I FEEL?

You already know that you can feel your thoughts. To Map insightfully and gain knowledge from your thoughts and questions you will need to be able to interpret your body responses and decipher those funny images that appear in your mind. In this chapter we are simply going to help you build on the skills you have already learnt.

If you start to find the exercise repetitive it is because you are becoming familiar with the skills. Before you know it, they will become automatic. Then you will be open to self-discoveries, which after all is what this book is about.

REMEMBER to read through the exercise first – or get a friend to talk you through it slowly – before you try it out.

**EXERCISE**
- Get comfy.
- Take three deep breaths.
- Close your eyes.

◆ Think of something wonderful – like a summer's day.

◆ Recognize how your body feels.

◆ Remember how a summer's day feels to you...

◆ *And* where this memory lives in your body.

Okay.

◆ Open your eyes.

◆ Take three deep breaths.

◆ Close your eyes again.

◆ In your mind ask yourself: 'Where do I feel... (Satisfaction, Happiness, etc.)... in my body?'

◆ Focus your attention on your body.

◆ Notice which part of your body responds to the question you just asked.

◆ Notice if you also get an image to go with the feeling.

◆ Notice how...(Satisfaction, Happiness, etc.)...feels.

◆ Make a mental note of everything.

◆ Open your eyes gently.

◆ Write the results down here or in your notebook...

.........................................................................................................

.........................................................................................................

.........................................................................................................

.........................................................................................................

Well done.

These are some of the things we would have expected you to notice:

• You hear or 'see' the question.

• You become aware of an area in your body because it gets hot, cold, tingly and so on.

• If you focus on the body feeling, the sensation grows and may move into another part of your body.

• You may smile, laugh or cry.

- Your breathing may become deeper or shallower.
- You will 'see' an image or colour in your mind, have a memory or create a fantasy.
- You can become very relaxed.

As repetition is part of the skill building process, please take the time to ask each of the following questions of yourself using the same method we've outlined above. Record your experiences carefully, because you will need them later. You can use the example below as a guideline. Try this:

### Question

Where do I feel courage?

### Answer

- In my chest – it feels as if my chest is expanding.
- I saw a picture of St George and the dragon.
- I heard a trumpet fanfare.
- I feel strong all over, as if I could tackle anything.
- My breathing is deep and fast.

Okay. Here's a different way of answering the same question.

### Question

Where do I feel courage?

### Answer

- In my chest, it feels as if my chest is expanding.
- I remember standing up to the school bully in the playground.

- I hear my friends praising me.
- I feel strong all over.
- I feel proud of myself.
- My breathing was deep and fast, now it has slowed down.

Now you try.

Read all the instructions first, then do this exercise.

**EXERCISE**

◆ Please ask yourself the following questions:
  - Where do I feel courage?
  - Where do I feel joy?
  - Where do I feel peace?
  - Where do I feel love?
◆ Try to be aware of the following:
  - Is this a fantasy or a memory?
  - Did I get an image or sound in my head?
  - How am I feeling now?
  - How long did the feeling last and how real was it?
◆ When you have finished, take a few minutes to relax. Make a cup of tea, go for a walk, get physical.

Hello again. How do you think you're doing? How far do you feel you've come?

Reviewing is a useful tool when you are learning any new skill so let's look at what you have achieved up to this point.

You have learnt:

☺ Self-assessment

☺ Being in reality

☺ To focus your attention in the present

☺ Honesty with yourself – and others

☺ Relaxation skills

☺ To focus on your body

☺ About tension – and recognizing and then releasing it

☺ Visualization

☺ Naming your feelings, wonderful and not so wonderful

☺ To feel feelings – 'tuning in' and how not to 'tune out'

☺ To think good, feel good

☺ Using your imagination in a positive way (creatively)

☺ To ask for feedback

☺ To recognize a problem if you have one

☺ To think good 'nourishing thoughts'

☺ To give yourself a good time...

Wow!

If you've made any self-discoveries, write them down; for example 'I can use imagery', 'I can relax', 'I can ask for help'.

.................................................................................................................

.................................................................................................................

.................................................................................................................

.................................................................................................................

If you feel you haven't quite mastered some of the skills above, make a note or ring them and just be aware that, at this stage, it's quite natural to feel a little uncertain. You will find that with practice, the skills will become second nature and soon you won't even notice how expert you've become.

You are now going to try something a little more challenging: expanding your self-questioning skills!

**EXERCISE**

◆ Ask yourself, in turn:

- How do *I feel* about animals, flowers, spring and so on?
- How do *I feel* about asking myself questions/being asked questions?
- How do *I feel* about what I've learnt so far?
- How do *I feel* about my appearance/clothes/car/home?

◆ If you begin to intellectualize or rationalize too much, focus your attention on the *italic* word, reaffirm the question, tune into feelings and try again.

Remember, it's that first, unconsidered response that's important, however silly, irrelevant or illogical you think it is. (We'd much rather you wrote down 'pink bananas' than 16 pages of superbly argued analysis.)

◆ Write your responses down – you'll almost certainly want to keep a record of your advance towards clarity!

**EXERCISE**

Now for another exercise along the same lines. See if you can spot what's subtly different from the last one.

◆ Ask yourself, in turn:

- What gives me pleasure?
- What makes me angry?
- What makes me excited?

Remember to use all the skills you have learnt:

   Relax, Focus, Feel, Record, Remember, Review.

*Just because something is uncomfortable doesn't mean you can't have a good feeling about it.*

*Why you've worked so hard*

# *9*

# WHY YOU'VE WORKED SO HARD

---

*If you want your seeds to flower, plant them in fertile ground.*

If you are wondering why you have had to work so hard at relaxing, developing your imagination and learning to recognize your emotions and feelings, it's because you unlearned all these skills when you were growing up. If you don't believe us just take a look at small children. They sleep when they are tired, demand food when they are hungry, laugh when they are happy and cry when they are sad.

As we get older, life becomes demanding and when faced with responsibility we can go into auto-pilot only feeling and expressing what is deemed acceptable. We often forget to ask for what we need, how to play, how to rest and how to be contented. We lose our dreams, forget our desires and get hooked on survival.

Well, we want you to remember!

Sure, living in the real world, the 'real' world as we tend to call it (often with gritted teeth), making do and making good are important. But so is your internal world. Remember 'When you think good you feel good'? Until you take the time to listen to your body and through it to your hopes and fears, you really won't know

---

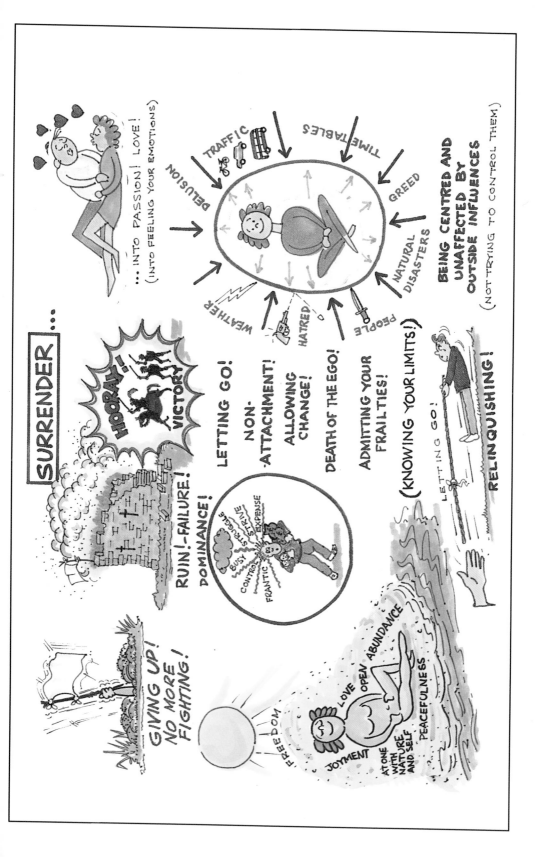

ECSTASY
LOVE
JOY
I'M UNDERSTOOD
I UNDERSTAND
FRIENDSHIP
& INTIMACY
PARTNERSHIP
ABUNDANCE
HOMECOMING
THIS IS WHERE
MY IS
FRUIT
FULL
ROOTED.

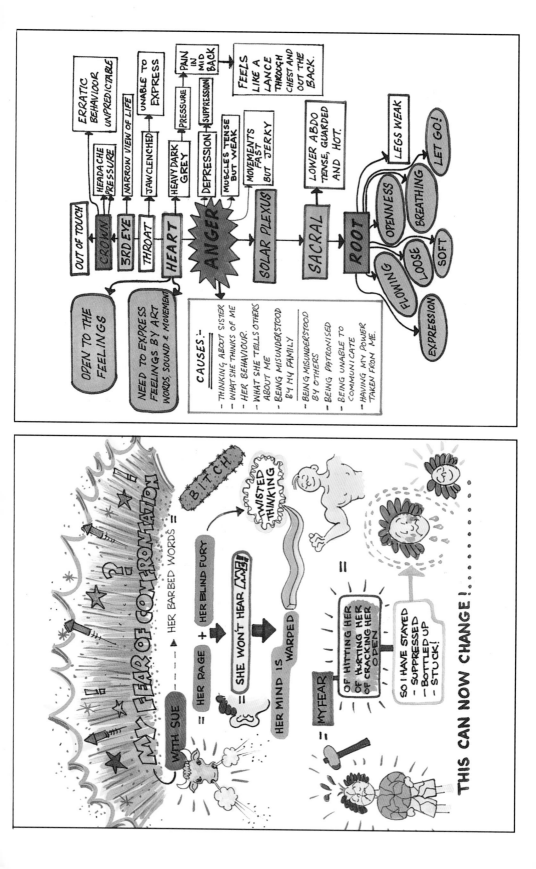

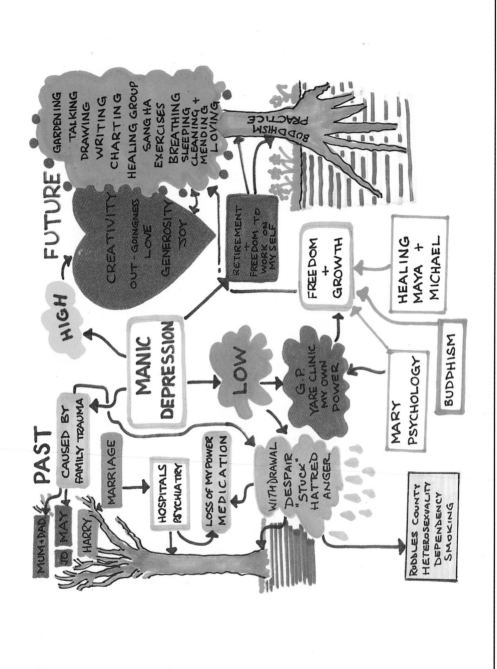

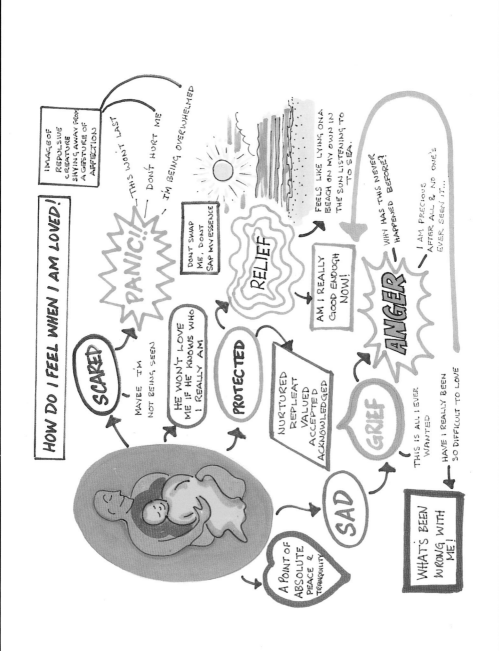

WHY DO I NEED RESCUING ?
IRRITATION
ANNOYANCE
RAGE
I DON'T NEED RESCUING
STOMP
STOMP
STOMP
I CAN LOOK AFTER MYSELF.
I DON'T NEED ANYONE
DEFIANCE
HOW DO YOU KNOW WHAT I FEEL ?
PUT THERE WHEN REJECTED IN THE PAST
NOBODY LOVES ME!
THEY WON'T LET ME BE ME!!
WAIL SOB SOB WAIL
HELP SAVE ME! SAVE ME!
HELPLESS WAIF-LIKE CREATURE IN THE PIT OF MY STOMACH
THIS TURNS TO THIS WHEN I'M NOT LISTENED TO
MOTHER
FATHER
"DON'T BE SO SILLY"
"OF COURSE YOU DON'T MEAN IT"
"SHUT UP & CALM DOWN OR I'LL SMACK YOU"
"NO YOU DON'T FEEL..."
THIS IS THE ONLY WAY I KNOW OF BEING HEARD (WHICH IS SAFE)
WHAT WOULD STOP ME NEEDING TO BE RESCUED?
-REAL LOVE-
-TOTAL ACCEPTANCE-
-NURTURING-

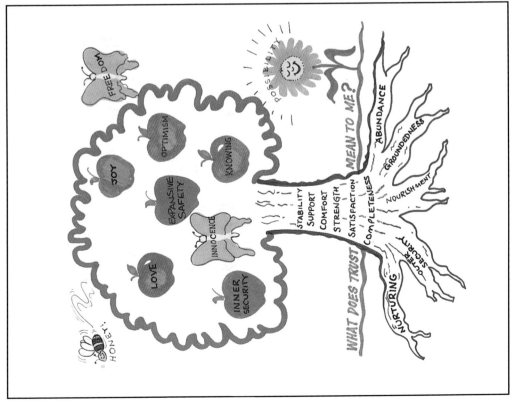

what you do or you don't want. Under these conditions it's likely that you will find yourself driven to achieving – or avoiding – the plans and expectations of society as a whole, parents or other major influencers.

*A wise person pleases himself.*

What would you give to be free from guilt, worry, anxiety, fear and pressure, free to live your dream? Would you be willing to give up the habit of feeling those emotions?

You are probably so used to living with these feelings that it seems impossible not to have them around all the time. Connecting with your feelings leads to freedom, freedom to honesty, and honesty to success.

Now that you have registered some of your life foundation skills we are going to show you how to capitalize on them through the skill of Emotional Mapping. Remember 'Bon Voyage'? Well the stores are laid in, the deck is scrubbed, the Martini is on ice and we are off on a trip around the harbour.

*A journey of a thousand miles starts from beneath one's feet.*

LAO-TZU

*Starting to Map*

# *10*

# STARTING TO MAP

---

*Our mission is to shine a light where none has shone before.*
CAPTAIN SPARRK, STARSHIP EVEREDDY
(with apologies!)

Congratulations!

Now you are ready to put all that hard work in the preceding chapters into practice. Your journey into yourself is about to begin.

To get you going, we've given you specially prepared Training Maps. They're so simple, they may remind you of a time in your childhood when you drew dot to dot or coloured by numbers. These Maps are only a beginning and will bear very little resemblance to what you will soon be producing in a few chapters' time, but bear with us for the moment.

So, let's begin.

First we need to tell you something about Emotional Mapping and how it works. Opposite is a simplified example of a Map. Look at it carefully and, if you'd like to, make notes.

---

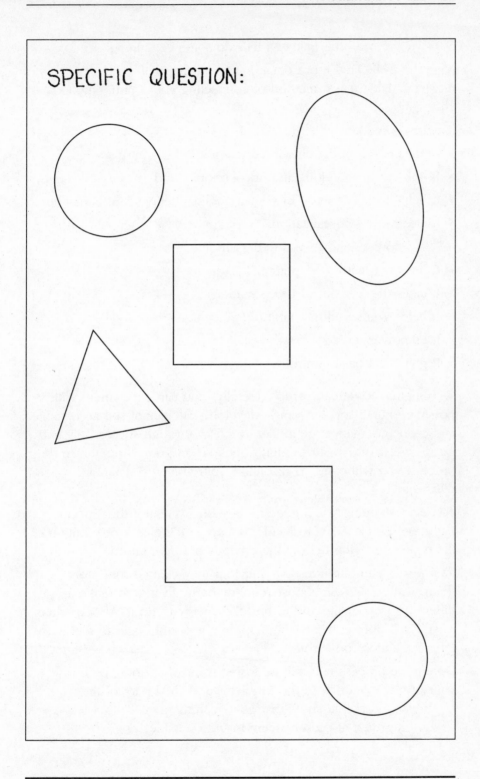

SPECIFIC QUESTION:

Now you've seen the imagery, let's do some explaining.

Mapping is a visual representation of your internal, emotional and mental activity. It is a method of connecting your mind, emotions and intuition.

It works something like this:

- It links mind, body, emotion and spirit.
- It links your conscious and unconscious mind.
- It helps to make sense of your thoughts, feelings and behaviour.
- It aids rapid self-realization.
- It develops tolerance and understanding.
- It links you with your potential.
- It takes the fear out of new situations.
- It helps you avoid the habit of struggling.
- It empowers you.
- It gives you back control.

With all this at your fingertips (literally) you can experiment with possible futures and outcomes, develop strategies of self-acceptance and change, enhance the ability to follow through successfully and build up a trust in your thoughts, feelings and development. In the process, you will come to recognize your ability to make a difference.

To begin Mapping you'll need a question. We call it the 'Specific Question'. Whatever you decide to Map, you'll gain a recognition of the real issues lying behind the obvious or apparent one.

As a result, your attitudes or behaviour may change subtly or dramatically. You will almost certainly be motivated to make a difference in your life and to find the energy to do it. After a while, as you get more familiar with Mapping, you will begin to feel more in control, more powerful.

During the process you will be losing something, too! You'll lose your preoccupation with the problems and shed a lot of the negativity and helplessness that goes with them. You'll get less upset about things that at present seem insurmountable.

Maps are simply records of behaviour. However, the process of Mapping and its results are quite challenging. It can be helpful to have a record of how the Map developed, your feelings while creating the Map and any other emotions, insights or mental shifts that you made during the process. So keep a pad by your side in case you want to jot down notes.

Okay. Let's begin!

From this moment on, you are an artist. The paper is your canvas and the subject is life – your life.

As an artist you'll need to be kitted out, so you'll need the following equipment:

- A variety of coloured pencils, crayons and felt-tips
- Blank sheets of unlined paper – lots of it and as big as possible. If you only have normal size writing paper (A4 for example) stick at least six of these together with adhesive tape (on the back – it's hard to draw over) to make one big sheet.
- A large table or floorspace
- Extra adhesive tape – just in case you really get carried away!
- A note pad to scribble on

Now to prepare your space:

◆ Take the phone off the hook or unplug it.

◆ See to the dog, cat or tortoise.

◆ Turn off the TV.

◆ Put on some of your favourite instrumental music (singing will distract you).

◆ If you like candles and/or incense, light some.

◆ Have a refreshing drink to hand.

◆ Get comfy in your favourite chair or with lots of cushions.

◆ Close your eyes and relax for a few minutes before looking at the Example Map opposite:

The Example Map is a visual representation of what can happen when someone relaxes; we'll call him John. If John were to do it again at another time, the map would probably look quite different.

This is how the map was made: In steps 1 to 4 John tuned into his body and how it felt, and into specific places as they came to his attention. He then went on to check how each part felt and recorded these on the map as follows:

### Head

**Q** How does my head feel?

**A**

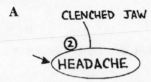

### Stomach

**Q** How does my stomach feel?

**A**

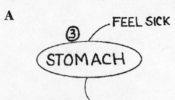

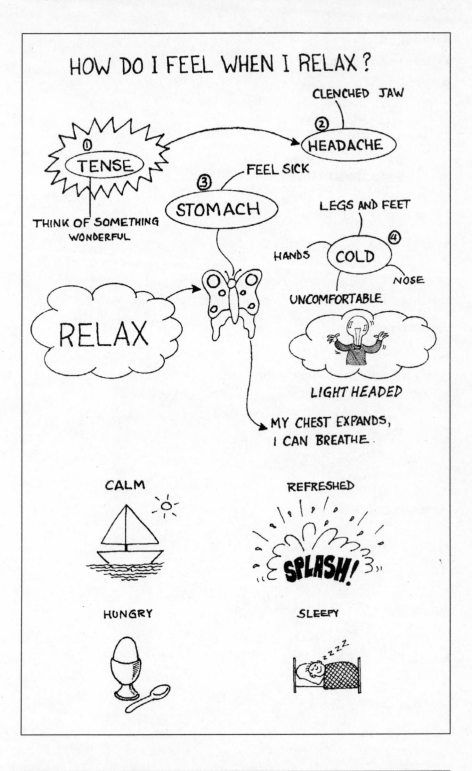

### Cold

**Q** Where do I feel cold?

**A**

Now that the initial responses were recorded, John began to ask questions that would help with filling in the details, like this:

### Tenseness

**Q** How can I stop myself from feeling tense?

**A** With a little reminding, John came up with thinking about something wonderful.

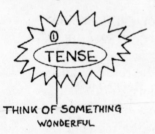

**Q** What happens when I think of something wonderful?

**A**

The next question was:

**Q** What happens when I start to relax?

**A**

MY CHEST EXPANDS,
I CAN BREATHE.

His next question was:

**Q** What is the result of having time to breathe and time to rest?

**A**

Look at the map again. As you can see, the result of all this introspection was a series of words and images on the page. John added lines and arrows to show which answers led to which. Then he wrote along the connecting lines so he'd remember how he'd made the link.

Next we're going to ask you to use a Training Map but, first, take a break, get physical and come back to us shortly.

So, get comfy again. Here goes:

◆ Take a fresh piece of paper. Decide on your 'Specific Question' and write it on the top of your Training Map. If you can't think of a question of your own, ask yourself 'How do I feel before and after I relax?'.

◆ Put your immediate responses into boxes and shapes – see the page opposite. Just let the shape suggest itself to you as being the best place to put your response. You don't have to fill in all the shapes but if you do and want more, just draw some of your own.

◆ Doodle as much as you need to.

◆ Take your crayons or pencils and fill the map in with colours you feel are appropriate. Remember to feel your response to each word or image first, before you fill it in.

◆ Focus on getting the responses down onto the page. The connections will come later.

◆ Relax! Enjoy it! Go wild with the colours!

◆ Remember to ask yourself questions like:

• How do I feel?

• How can I change it?

• What do I do when...?

• What can I do about...?

• What happens when...?

• Why do I...?

• Why is it that...?

• Why does this feel so important?

• When do I...?

• When does this happen?

• When can this change?

• Where do I feel...?

• Am I happy with the result?

And also...

What do I recognize/see in my map at this point?

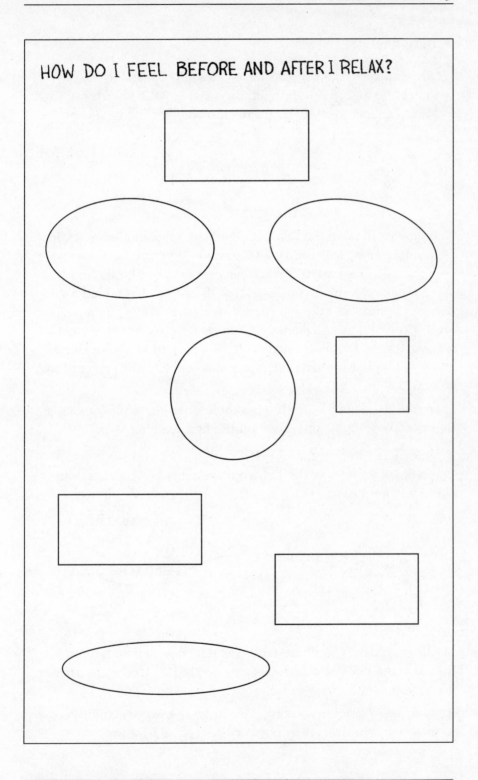

HOW DO I FEEL BEFORE AND AFTER I RELAX?

◆ Have fun!

> Note: You can't make a mistake. Anything goes, so feel free to
> scribble, doodle, paint and think in images. Be five years old
> again! Don't read any further until you've completed the chart.

Now you've filled in the first Training Map, take another quick look
at Example Map No 1 on page 00 to remind yourself about
connections. This part of the Mapping process can be the most
enlightening. We think you'll find that the colour has added a new
dimension and that you will connect with the process on a deeper
level. However, as enlightenment can be a bit elusive sometimes,
we suggest the following method for learning to join your shapes.
(We're sorry, but we can't offer you numbers to follow as each map
is individual to you!).

However, try asking yourself this simple question while looking at
the responses you've put down on the first Training Map:

• How are these two words connected?

You will get an answer through your thoughts and feelings, which
could be like this:

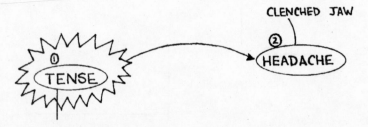

In other words: 'When I am tense I experience muscle tension in
my back and neck which results in a headache.' Hence the arrow
going from 'Tense' to 'Headache'.

If no answer comes, try asking: 'Are these two words connected?' or
'If these two words were connected, how would I know?'

◆ Please complete your Training Map now.

◆ Once you feel you have completed it, put it to one side and do something quite different for a while. Look at it again in a couple of hours or even tomorrow and then see if you would like to add anything to it.

So, for the meantime, that's your first Mapping lesson! Well done!

Now that you've successfully completed your first Map, draw some more blank Training Maps, *see* the example at the end of this chapter and practise Mapping how you *feel* and how you *respond* to certain questions or circumstances. Again, you might find it useful to copy them. It's probably too early to take on a major issue or problem, so for the moment, stick to practising on fairly straightforward issues. Once you are comfortable with the basic techniques of Mapping, you can develop your skill and look at the really deep and insightful stuff.

Meanwhile, here is that list of questions again, to use while you are getting familiar with Mapping:

• How do I feel?
• How can I change it?
• What do I do when...?
• What can I do about...?
• What happens when...?
• Why do I...?
• Why is it that...?
• Why does this feel so important?
• When do I...?
• When does this happen?
• When can this change?
• Where do I feel...?
• Am I happy with the result?

And also...

• What do I recognize/see in my map at this point?

Good luck! Enjoy the process and – remember – keep practising. Contrary to popular belief, practice won't make you perfect but it will turn you into a very good Mapper.

You'll find that, when you are Mapping more than everyday issues, you'll hear inner voices and feel new things, things that may be rather challenging. We'll talk about these in the next chapters.

Finally, we'd like to remind you that the *process* of Mapping is as important as the *results* or *insights* that you gain. Truth is a personal thing and, moreover, is constantly changing, so results are often of momentary importance or significance, although all your discoveries will contribute to the expanding mosaic of your self-knowledge.

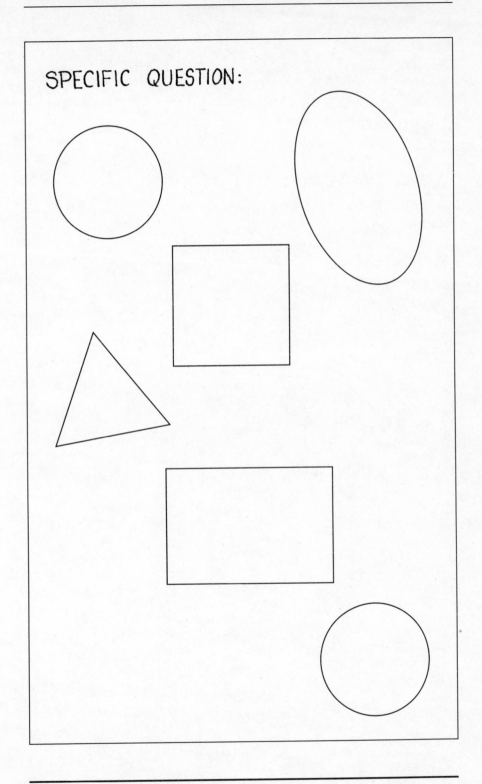

SPECIFIC QUESTION:

## *Chattering Monkeys*

# *11*

# CHATTERING MONKEYS

Childhood is a time of wonder and confusion, of experiment and conclusion. Children are open and impressionable, their map of the world is waiting to be coloured by life's experience. (The only trouble is they don't usually get to choose the palette, the brushes or the quality of the paper.) They absorb the colour indiscriminately, and the more emotionally charged the experience the more the map changes and the thicker the covering of paint.

Deeply felt emotion becomes a belief, a silent voice we hear in our heads; and these voices shape our landscapes, the territory in which we live and how we feel about it.

We have called these voices 'Chattering Monkeys'. They sit perched comfortably on our shoulders reinforcing the reflections of all the people that influenced us (for good or bad) while we were growing up. Whatever the tone, these voices are compelling; we listen and respond.

Chattering Monkeys can stop you from making foolish choices and protect you in unfamiliar situations by delivering a few well-placed doubts or reminders. However, they can also prevent you from charting new and abundant waters by taking the wind out of your sails.

They come in many different guises – mother, father, pirate, priest – and go by many different names – critic, task-master, ship's captain, moralist. To illustrate the point please read this typical (and familiar?) Chattering Monkey Script. You may want to get creative with the casting and give the CM role to the reproachful people in your life.

THE SCENE   It's the weekend. You are on your own on a long car journey, travelling through remote and unfamiliar countryside. Night is drawing in, it's getting colder and you begin to sense that something is wrong with the car. You drive on but then ... (*cue dramatic music and the sound of approaching thunder and lightning*) ... the car shudders to a halt. (*Cue terminal grinding sounds*)

|  |  |  |
|---|---|---|
|  | YOU | Damn, I'm going to be late. |
| (Critic) | CM | You should have stopped at that last service station. |
|  | YOU | I wonder where the nearest phone is? |
| (Mocker) | CM | Probably at the last service station! |
|  | YOU | I wonder how far back that last service station was? |
| (Drama Queen) | CM | Miles away! You'll be walking all night. Everyone's going to be worrying about you and wondering where you are. Why didn't you stop at the last service station? |

YOU    I wish I'd stopped at that last service station! Now I'm going to be late, everyone will be worrying about me and they won't know where I am. I hope they don't worry too much. I wonder where I can get some help? There must be a phone box somewhere.

(Judge)    CM    You are so stupid sometimes! Public phones never work – they're always vandalized!

*(Cue sound of breaking glass and plastic)*

YOU    I hope I can find a phone that works. I'll start walking back to that last village. There must be a bar or something. I hope I find something open.

(Knowall)    CM    No chance! You know what it's like on a Sunday. Everything closes early. This isn't the big city, you know.

YOU    Everything will be shut by the time I get there. I'll have to walk back to that service station but that will probably be shut too and the phone will be broken.

(Disabler)    CM    You'll never make it in those flimsy shoes. Besides, they don't let strangers into service stations late at night because they're frightened of being robbed. You'd better stay here.

YOU    I bet they don't let strangers use the service station phone. Perhaps they'll think I'm going to rob the place. I hope I don't meet any strange people on the road. I wonder if I should leave my wallet in the car? But they will probably break into it anyway.

*(Cue more breaking glass and plastic)*

NARRATOR    To be continued...

*(Cue commercial for mobile phones)*

With all this contrary feedback is it any wonder that our intrepid traveller gave in to his confusion, threw in the towel and stayed put?

When you are not exactly sure what to do and when the thing that you are facing could be a danger or a possibility, (be it the Bermuda Triangle – lots of uncertain potential in there, or Bali Hi – remember *South Pacific*) you can be sure that those irritating Monkeys will turn up the volume.

So how do we handle these undermining voices? How do we get past the emotion to that feeling insightful voice within?

**INSTRUCTION**

◆ Close your eyes.

◆ Be still. Be open.

◆ Think of something wonderful.

*Thoughts on thinking*

# 12

# THOUGHTS ON THINKING

---

*He who knows others is wise.*
*He who knows himself is enlightened.*

LAO TZU

We know that if you have done the exercises in the book so far (rather than just read about them) you will have discovered something. That is, that tiny impulses in your brain – thoughts – carry you across life's ocean. Profound certainly, exciting definitely but, (and this is where you may be wishing you had a life jacket) without maps, a sextant, a compass or a rudder you are at the mercy of the wind and the tides. You never know if you are going to end up on a treasure island or dashed on the rocks!

So what can you do about it? How can you regain control, take the helm, become the captain of your ship and the master of your destiny?

We believe that understanding how thoughts work will give you the tools with which to craft an effective future. So we have defined, classified and categorized and this is what we came up with.

Thought can be broken down in the following ways.

---

## *Active Thinking*

This tends to be directed by your *conscious waking mind*. It is the type of thought that you are aware of. It is directed by a need to discover, recognize, make sense of, order and define. It is deliberate. Examples of active thinking are:

- writing a shopping list
- planning a route from home to the airport
- doing your taxes
- having a conversation
- expressing an idea

It is often linear and sequential and even when it is illogical it has a 'left-brain', logical impetus.

## *Passive Thinking*

This is that constant stream of words and images that appear in your mind when you are doing something else – like washing the dishes, driving your car or staring out of the classroom window during maths. When you think passively you experience a series of apparently random images with a soundtrack, rather like a film, although the overall movie seems disjointed; one image triggers another, but the links are often too fast or too obscure for us to make sense of.

These passive thoughts can be intrusive, distracting, diverting, preoccupying, irrational, disturbing, even terrifying. Passive Thinking is constant and can only be shut down once you become aware of it.

*Note* At times like these you can use Active Thinking as a pacifier, and as a way of 'controlling' your mind.

However, Passive Thinking can also be pleasant, a kind of mental pottering, allowing the thoughts to meander around and – if you let them – take you with them on a magical mystery tour of the mind. In this way, Passive Thinking can be refreshing and restorative.

It's also contemplative and good for integrating experiences or events such as:

- Remembering your first love
- Learning to drive or some other new skill

- A news item on TV
- Something someone told you about a good friend
- Bad news
- A profound realization
- The unresolved argument you had with Uncle Fred
- Mapping

## Positive/Negative Thinking

### Negative Thinking

Negative Thinking sounds something like this:

☹ Nobody loves me.

☹ I will never be able to do that.

☹ I'm sure he won't phone.

☹ I'm too tired to...

☹ I'm too fat to get fit and I can't stick to diets.

☹ If I stand up for myself he'll leave me.

Negative thinking leaves you:

☹ deflated

☹ sad

☹ insecure

☹ guilty

☹ confused

☹ manic

☹ frustrated

☹ disempowered

It is:

☹ lazy

☹ undermining

☹ self-negating

☹ dangerous

It creates fear which leads to:

🙁 a downward cycle

🙁 depression

🙁 struggle

🙁 blame

🙁 paralysis

🙁 pessimism

For many of us it is also a habit, a thoroughly learnt and conditioned response to the rollercoaster we call Life.

We *expect* to think negative. We even joke about it and have developed Murphy's Law to 'prove' that if something can go wrong, it will. To counteract Murphy it has become fashionable to 'Think Positive'.

### *Positive Thinking*

The theory behind positive thinking is that you can 'talk' yourself into anything. That you can take any problem or any issue and just change it. That you can wash your brains of all the stuff that you no longer need. Life will then be wonderful, goes the theory, you will have everything you could possibly want and you will want for nothing. We are led to believe that we can simply think ourselves:

☺ into a better job

☺ into the perfect relationship

☺ out of trouble

☺ thin

☺ rich

☺ fit

We agree that *how you think* plays an important part in whether you will succeed in your ambitions but Positive Thinking is not the all-purpose panacea that many would have you believe.

Positive thinking works something like this:

John is financially compromised, with outgoings exceeding income and getting deeper into debt. He picks up a book on positive thinking, thinks it's a great idea and spends hours, days and weeks affirming: 'I am wealthy, I am rich, I can have everything.' This makes him feel much better about his situation and he knows that everything is going to be all right because he is a positive thinker. 'Everything is fine', he tells himself, as he is evicted from his home. His friends look on with a mixture of disbelief and sympathy saying: 'It's all been too much for him, he's lost his marbles, he just can't seem to get a grip on reality.' And what does John say? 'You guys just don't understand, you're being negative. I'm just getting rid of things I no longer need. This house wasn't right for me anyway. I can have everything. I just have to think harder.'

So what actually happened here? John knew he had a problem, so he got positive and ended up homeless.

> *Thoughts without actions build castles in the air. Look out for falling debris!*

John just didn't realize that he was only using *one* of the tools in his toolbox. His vision for himself didn't come true because he *thought* change without *acting* as if something had changed. *He got positive without being proactive.* He didn't know about:

**The Rules of Change**

☺ Be real, be honest.

☺ Check how reality feels.

☺ Think about how you want to be.

☺ Check how your potential future feels.

☺ Think about a strategy for change.

☺ Check that the strategy feels okay.

☺ Get proactive – implement it.

☺ Be focused and positive in the thoughts and actions towards your goal.

Spot the difference?

Becoming aware and real takes time, effort and commitment. However, the results are so encouraging that most people we know, once they have experimented, happily swap the habits of negative thinking and lazy, undermining passive thinking for a more proactive approach.

Negative Thinking and Positive Thinking are mind sets that are literally worlds apart and in order to get from one to the other you will need some kind of mechanism to span the gap. We suggest *compassion* as it takes the judgement out of your thoughts and opens the door which leads towards an objective and tolerant reality.

Here is an example of an exercise that we use during workshops to help people move from one state of thinking to another.

| Old Thought | Compassionate Thought | Positive Thought |
| --- | --- | --- |
| I'm really stupid | I don't understand yet | I'm brilliant |
| Life stinks | Life is challenging right now | Life's wonderful |
| I can't do it | I don't know if I can but I'll try | I can do it |
| Dad always shouts at me | Dad shouts when he gets angry | I know Dad loves me |
| I'm trapped in this marriage | My marriage is broken and I don't know how to fix it | I can have a great marriage |

Okay, now it's your turn to practise how you can 'Change Your Mind'. Use the first column to write down your normal everyday thoughts about yourself and life, then follow the example above, and see how compassionate and positive you can become. If you need some more space, write in your notebook.

| Old Thought | Compassionate Thought | Positive Thought |
| --- | --- | --- |
| ............................. | ............................. | ............................. |
| ............................. | ............................. | ............................. |
| ............................. | ............................. | ............................. |
| ............................. | ............................. | ............................. |
| ............................. | ............................. | ............................. |

Well done; every time you find yourself thinking badly of yourself (or anyone else for that matter), take a deep breath, think of something wonderful and 'change' your mind!

*When walking through life's bog, wear a gas mask.*

*Guardian Angels*

# 13

# GUARDIAN ANGELS

Within the realms of your mind lives a peaceful voice. It talks to you almost as much as your Chattering Monkeys. You forget that it's there because you don't always hear it. It's not that it is particularly quiet, it's just that you and your monkeys are particularly noisy!

Unlike the monkeys it doesn't follow you around, it doesn't need to. Its presence pervades your life. It is your personal all-knowing, all-seeing, all-compassionate, all-weather best friend.

This 'Guardian Angel', as we like to call it, goes by many other names: Guide, Higher-Self, Master, Teacher, Superconscious, God Within and Great White Spirit to coin but a few. Take your pick. There is no great secret in connecting with it, you just need *peace and quiet*.

So straight away we have a problem, right? Not only do you lead a busy life but ... all those Chattering Monkeys.

There is a solution. You have the knowledge and the ability, we have the technique, so let's go into partnership.

As always, read the following exercise through from beginning to end before you try it. Enjoy the trip!

**EXERCISE**

- Prepare your space.
- Do the phone/dog routine (by now the dog will be getting seriously concerned – or seriously fit).
- Get comfy.
- Close your eyes.
- Think of something wonderful.
- Breathe!
- Relax for a couple of minutes and breathe light into your body.

(Now comes the new bit)

- Focus your attention about six inches above the top of your head.
- Move all your attention to that spot.
- Notice how your body feels.
- Relax in the sensation and in the silence for a couple of minutes.

You are now connected to your Guardian Angel.

- Focus your attention on your hands and feet.
- Take a very deep breath.
- Draw your attention back to your body.
- Breathe deeply and stretch.
- Open your eyes and look around.
- Remain sitting for about a minute.
- Write down below what happened.

.........................................................................................................

.........................................................................................................

.........................................................................................................

.........................................................................................................

.........................................................................................................

.........................................................................................................

These are the kinds of things we would expect to have happened – but not all or even all at once!

- It was harder to relax.
- You kept wondering what was going to happen.

As you shifted your attention above your head:

- You felt waves moving up through your body.
- You became very still.
- Your thoughts quietened down.
- You felt sensations in your head.
- You felt much lighter or as if you were floating.
- Your body 'disappeared'.
- You saw colours or images in your mind, rather like when dreaming.
- Your stomach flipped.
- You nodded off!
- You felt very peaceful.
- You got relaxed but none of the above happened and you are wondering why.

Good, that was a great first try!

Connecting with your Guardian Angel for the first time is rather like a first chance meeting with someone you feel attracted to. Building a relationship with it takes willingness, time and practice. Becoming familiar with it will only take openness and the ability to share.

We have found that people become quite attached to this caring part of themselves. Along with pleasant body feelings, they may get images of 'angelic' beings which they then like to name, as this helps to build familiarity.

Okay. Now go back to that part of yourself again, follow the instructions below and begin to build up a sense of the qualities or personality of your Guardian Angel.

- Prepare your space.
- Phone/dog/plumber.

- Get comfy.
- Close your eyes and breathe.
- Relax for a couple of minutes and breathe light into your body.
- Focus your attention about six inches above the top of your head.
- Move all your attention to that spot.
- Notice how your body feels.
- You are now connected to the Guardian Angel. Take a couple of minutes to get to know it a little better... and then
- Focus your attention on your hands and feet.
- Breathe deeply and stretch.
- Open your eyes and look around.
- Remain sitting for about a minute.
- Write down below what happened.

........................................................................................................................

........................................................................................................................

........................................................................................................................

........................................................................................................................

........................................................................................................................

If, after you've done all these exercises, you're still having a problem with your noisy Chattering Monkeys, and listening to your Guardian Angel is a bit like trying to hear the sound of daisies growing on the edge of an airport runway, try this:

**EXERCISE**

- Close your eyes.
- Imagine you have a radio dial in your head.
- Tune it to the Chattering Monkey.
- Turn the volume down, make it comfortable but not intrusive.
- Now tune in to your Guardian Angel frequency.

◆ Move your attention to 6 inches above your head.

◆ Turn the volume up.

Well done! Now get up and make yourself a coffee, go for a walk or get physical. Reassure the dog. Come back to us later.

During workshops the commonest question we are asked is: 'How do I really know when my Guardian Angel is talking to me?' or 'How will I know the difference between my Chattering Monkeys and my Guardian Angel?' The answers to these questions can be found by doing the following exercises, one after the other, taking notes as you go along.

### FIRST EXERCISE

◆ Choose one of the questions below to work with or, if none of them fits your particular circumstances, make one up that suits you, along similar lines.

- Why don't I have a boyfriend/girlfriend?

- Should I change my job?

- How can I make more money?

- Why is life such a struggle?

- Should I end my relationship?

- How can I give up cigarettes/alcohol/overeating?

- How can I make my dreams come true?

◆ Now, please do the exercise right now with no preparation, as follows.

◆ Write – My chosen question is:

........................................................................................................

◆ Write – The first answer I got was:

........................................................................................................

◆ Write – What do I think about the answer?

..............................................................................................................

◆ Write – How do I feel about the answer?

..............................................................................................................

**SECOND EXERCISE:**

◆ Write the same question that you chose for the last exercise.

My Chosen Question is:

..............................................................................................................

◆ Now follow these instructions, but read them through at least once before you begin.

◆ Get comfy.

◆ Take three deep breaths with closed eyes.

◆ Relax for a couple of minutes.

◆ Open your eyes and read your question.

◆ Write down your answer and responses to it:

This time, the answer to my question is:

..............................................................................................................

What do I feel about my answer?

..............................................................................................................

What do I think about my answer?

..............................................................................................................

Good. That's great. Now before you start Exercise 3 get up, stretch and prepare your space (phone off the hook, quiet music, incense if you like it, you know by now what to do!). Read through the instructions at least once before you begin.

**THIRD EXERCISE:**

◆ Write down your question (yes, the same one as before!):

My Chosen Question is:

..............................................................................................................

- ◆ Get comfy.
- ◆ Think of something wonderful.
- ◆ Breathe and relax with eyes closed for a couple of minutes.
- ◆ Focus your attention to about 6 inches above your head.
- ◆ Without forcing it, allow your attention to intensify on that spot.
- ◆ Settle into the sensations for about a minute.
- ◆ Open your eyes and read your question.
- ◆ Close your eyes again and feel and listen to the answer for a few seconds.
- ◆ Open your eyes and write your answer and your responses to it.

My answer was:

..................................................................................................

..................................................................................................

How do I feel about my answer?

..................................................................................................

..................................................................................................

What do I think about my answer?

..................................................................................................

..................................................................................................

The experience was:

..................................................................................................

..................................................................................................

Well done. Take a break and come back to us in about five minutes.

Okay. This is what we would expect to have happened.

In Exercise 1 you may have:

- Heard something you already knew
- Criticized yourself for feeling that way
- Made excuses for yourself or someone else
- Said 'What if' or 'But' more than once
- Felt uncertain, fearful, confused, frustrated, anxious
- Thought: 'I don't know' at least once
- Told yourself: 'I can't do it' or 'It's impossible' at least once

In Exercise 2 you may have:

- Felt more relaxed and less anxious than during Exercise 1
- Had a clearer sense of the question or of the answer
- Felt more comfortable about the answer but not sure about the logistics
- Felt that the goal was out of your reach
- Heard 'What if' or 'If only' at least once
- Felt uncertain about your commitment
- Wondered what other people might think

In Exercise 3 you may have:

- Felt much more relaxed and secure in yourself
- Felt peaceful
- Had a pleasant physical response to both the question and the answer
- Felt the answer rather than thought it
- Felt good about what you saw and heard even though it might have surprised you
- Felt confused from time to time about how you were going to achieve your goal but still sure of the goal in spite of the feelings
- Felt motivated to follow through with your ideas
- Been surprised by the lack of mental resistance to the answer
- Been surprised by the depth of relaxation that you reached

- Been much happier with the result than in Exercises 1 and 2
- Had an emotional reaction to the answer and release such as tears or laughter (or both) and felt much better afterwards.

You will have noticed that the quality of your answers changed as you became more relaxed and less preoccupied with the question. During Exercises 2 and 3 your focus of attention was on yourself, not on the problem. Self-focus is a very important step in making successful life-changing decisions. When you self-focus you are in touch with the heart of the problem and you can approach it with love, understanding and respect.

The more you work in this way, the more you will be able to still the voices of the Chattering Monkeys and hear and respond to the voice of your Guardian Angel.

*Warning!* Those Chattering Monkeys are likely to be waiting for you to finish the exercise.

Although the imagery we have conjured up for your Chattering Monkeys can be comical, remember that the impact they have on your life is less than funny. There is more that you can and will have to do in order to manage and contain the influence they have over you.

They are stubborn little folk and it will take self-awareness and a degree of discipline to negate the influence they have over you. So, when that persistent chattering voice clamours for your attention, take a moment to use your visualization skills. Pop a large fruity lollipop into your Monkey's mouth (to quieten it down) and sit it in front of a video of *Chitty Chitty Bang Bang* to keep it happy.

*Intuition*

# 14

# INTUITION

*Learn to be silent. Let your quiet mind listen and absorb.*

PYTHAGORAS

Intuition. What is it?

A moment of inspiration.

A message from your Guardian Angel.

A feeling of deep knowing about something which hasn't happened yet.

So, is it valid or not?

Remember those times in your life when you just felt that 'something' (either good or bad) was going to happen? Like that feeling you got just before a fight broke out in the bar; knowing which horse was going to win the Derby; or that time when you answered the phone and found yourself saying 'I was just about to call you'. We call this alertness 'having a hunch'. Hunches are a vital tool in our self-defence and self-realization kit.

We can get uncomfortable about intuition because the message we receive arrives without any apparent thought or input. Things are not supposed to be so easy, and when we are offered something for free we find ourselves being suspicious and wondering what the catch is.

Well, intuition comes with only one catch. As soon as you begin to question it or doubt its validity, it disappears. Often confusion takes its place. We want you to have clarity, so ponder on this.

Intuition is invaluable when you are journeying into yourself. A word here or an apparently random connection there will always make the difference between finding the source of your problem (and developing a healthy solution) and going round and round in ever-decreasing circles.

Have a look at the mazes below. They illustrate the difference between a Chattering Monkey decision, a Guardian Angel decision and an intuitive flash.

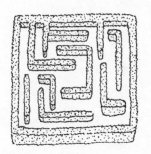 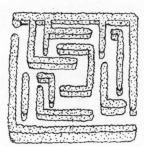 

We are not asking you to believe us, just to suspend your cynicism, so when you are Mapping, however trivial, silly or illogical you find your thoughts or feelings to be, put them down on your piece of paper. We know you'll be surprised at the result.

*Fear*

# 15

# FEAR

Overcome fear and you need overcome nothing else.

**fear** (*n.*) **1.** painful emotion caused
by impending danger **2.** a state of
alarm, dread or anxiety.

Now you're getting deeper into Mapping territory, it's likely that you will experience intense feelings of excitement, anticipation, pleasure, challenge and resolution. In this chapter, we will be discovering how fear shapes the landscape of your mind.

When we experience fear it may not express itself through the classic symptoms of shaking hands or rivulets of perspiration. However fear can appear as or feel like jealousy, anger, guilt, impatience, frustration, inconsistency, dishonesty, procrastination, stubbornness, humour, possessiveness, fanaticism, worry, overeating, smoking, or alcohol or drug abuse.

**Ask yourself this: If life is a school how do we get the most out of the lesson?**

What does fear have to teach us? For the answer, let's look at our ancestors. They had to put up with some pretty awesome natural disasters like an occasional ice-age, the odd volcanic eruption and the great flood. Not only that, they never knew if they would have dinner or be dinner that evening.

Realizing there was safety in numbers (if you roam the plains in a herd of buffalo, the wolf may not see you), they got together and started to form communities. These turned into societies, cultures, religions, empires and nations. Through fear we learned to co-operate and to live together.

To live successfully in these large human groups, you need to agree to rules. These are designed to protect us from conflict with each other and outsiders, and if the worst does happen, they give us a framework in which to resolve disputes. Another benefit of rules is that they give definition, whether it be national (borders or boundaries) or personal (roles and responsibilities). And last but not least, they create continuity and safety. Safety is, of course, important but it can lead to stagnation and is often used as an obstacle to change.

And here is the paradox. We are successfully innovative because of our natural curiosity and our ability to assess, adapt to and embrace change. And yet change is seen as a threat to our stability. So what is the answer?

You need to be able to trust that you can look after yourself in an environment that is constantly changing. You need to be 'fear-less' rather than 'fear-full'.

*A person who sees fear and walks towards it is ready to receive his or her heart's desire.*

What about you? How can you learn to convert fear from an obstacle into an opportunity, or a vehicle for growth? The answer comes once again from knowing yourself so let's get into some self-exploration.

## INSTRUCTION

◆ Prepare your space.

◆ Get your pens, paper and so on together.

◆ Do the phone/dog thing.

◆ Get comfy and breathe deeply.

◆ Relax for a few minutes with your eyes closed.

Now for some Mapping.

Ask yourself the question below and immediately Map your response on a Training Map.

*When I am frightened, how do I behave?*

Okay. How did you get on? Here is an example of someone else's responses. They realized through this the link between fear, anger and smoking, a habit they had been trying to break for some time.

Please take a little break now, because there's more of this. We know it can be a bit scary, but that's alright. Go as deep as you feel comfortable with but, remember, it's always possible to go deeper. There's no seabed in the complex geography of your mind, just huge, imponderable paradoxes waiting to be woken and, yes, more questions.

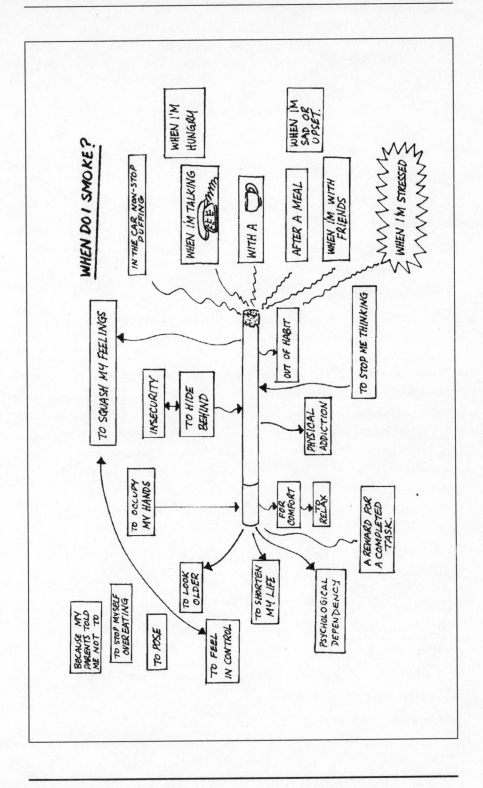

Hello again! If you didn't take a rest, you'll pay for it later. So, do as you're told – (please!).

- Prepare your space.
- Gather your equipment together – you know, pens, pencils, etc.
- Do the phone/dog thing.
- Get comfy.
- Breathe!
- Relax for a few minutes with your eyes closed.
- Open your eyes.
- Ask yourself this question and immediately Map your response on a Training Map:

*How would I behave if I wasn't frightened?*

How did that go? The sorts of responses we would have expected would be along the lines of those shown opposite:

If you look carefully at the examples of Fear we have shown so far, you will have noticed a recurrent theme – loss. Losing something that you are attached to like love, property, status or approval is very unpleasant, and as we are often compelled to avoid discomfort, we can and do use fear as a motivator. There is nothing like a looming deadline to help you to focus your attention on completing the job at hand.

In what areas of your life do you use fear as a motivator. What do you fear losing?

Yep! It's time for another Map!

Opposite you'll see someone else's Map on that subject. Have a look at it and then do your own.

Okay. Now it's your turn. What are you afraid of losing?

- Prepare your space
- Gather your equipment together – you know: pens, pencils, etc.
- Do the phone/dog thing.
- Get comfy.

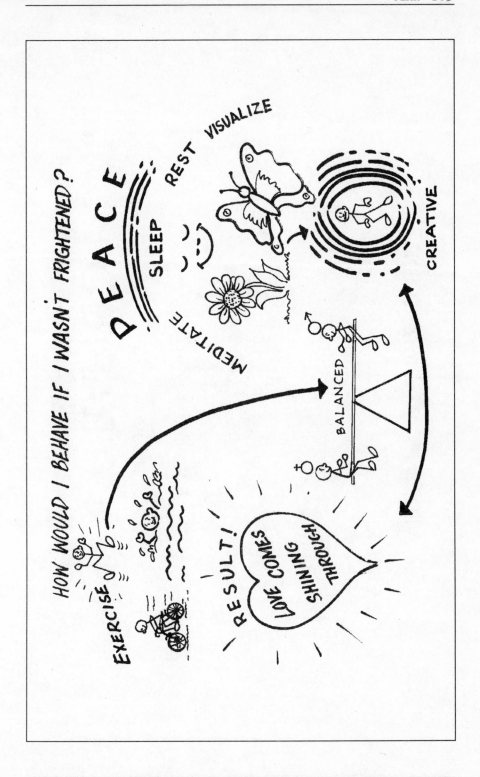

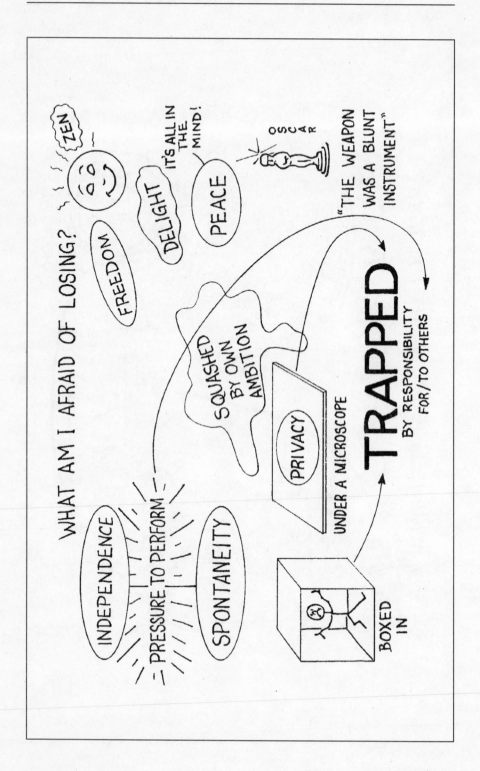

- ◆ Breathe!
- ◆ Relax for a few minutes with your eyes closed.
- ◆ Open your eyes.
- ◆ Ask yourself this question and immediately Map your response on a Training Map:

*What am I afraid of losing?*

How did that go? Now take each of the responses from the Map you've just done and ask about each in turn:

*How do I feel about losing...?*

Now, having done that, ask for each of your responses:

*When I'm in fear about losing..., how do I behave?*

Okay. Last one for the moment. Now Map:

*If I wasn't afraid of losing..., how would I behave?*

Good. Now take a break and come back to us after you've done something physical.

Now for a final exercise on Fear. Read it through first.

- ◆ Prepare your space.
- ◆ Do the phone/dog thing.
- ◆ Get comfy.
- ◆ Close your eyes.
- ◆ Breathe!
- ◆ Relax for a few minutes.
- ◆ Identify where in your body you feel fear about something.
- ◆ Breathe!
- ◆ Think of something wonderful.
- ◆ Isolate that wonderful feeling and move it slowly into the space where you feel the fear.

◆ Hold it there gently for a few moments.

◆ Let it go and slowly open your eyes.

This exercise will result in the fear being either balanced or counteracted. When you put something wonderful into the fear space, it becomes less fearful and you become more fear-less. After a bit of practice, you'll be able to use this technique when you are actually in fearful situations – but perhaps not always closing your eyes!

It *is* possible to choose excitement and enthusiasm over fear. And, as you become familiar with your fear landscape, the mountains will crumble, leaving a clear path.

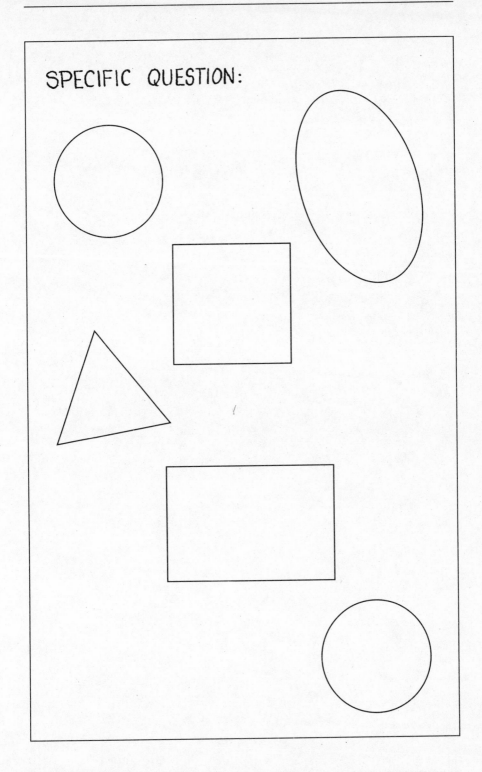

*Trust*

# *16*

# TRUST

---

*Be realistic: plan for a miracle.*
BHAGWAN SHREE RAJNEESH

Ultimately, the only person you can really trust is yourself. Sure, friends and family can help when things get tough, but fundamentally you are the one that has to live with yourself, and you are the one that has to maintain the motivation that gets you from A to B. So, how do you do it?

You will have already had a direct experience of your inner voice, and you know how it feels. This connection with your Guardian Angel is an 'open line' through which you can have an honest, frank, non-judgemental chat with the one person that really counts, *you*. The line will never be busy and you won't get a bill each quarter.

Remember to allow yourself time to be peaceful as stillness of mind and body deepens the connection. As it develops, you will acquire a sense of richness from your own opinions, thoughts and judgements. The more you master trusting, the more you wonder how you lived without it. Self-respect and self-recognition soon follow. Self-love won't be far behind.

Loving yourself means you always have the courage and the ability to let go of your doubt. You lose the need to know exactly what the

---

future holds and you finally relax. Relaxation frees energy, whether it is inside or outside your body. Energy then flows freely around and through you. You become a space for opportunity, the world is your oyster and the possibilities are as limitless as the stars in the sky.

Look at the map on trust. It was completed immediately after a period of quiet meditation.

Now take some time out for yourself. Do the phone/dog thing and ask yourself the following questions. Take your time, the answers may surprise you and you will need time to contemplate and integrate the answers.

- What is the benefit of trust in my life?
- How can I develop my ability to trust myself?
- What is it that I need to do to become more trusting?
- What will my life look like when I have learnt to trust?

# CONCLUSION

We hope you have enjoyed sharing this part of your life's journey with us, and that you have found *A to Zen* a useful guidebook. While travelling with us you will have begun to perceive yourself in a new way. Perhaps you now understand better the whys and wherefores of your behaviour and have learnt through experience and by paying attention to yourself that what you believe, or lead yourself to believe, creates a map for your consciousness to follow. Whatever you now know or have rediscovered, you have created an all-terrain vehicle that will help you to negotiate life's ups and downs.

Remember that, however well you plan your route, there will always be surprises. Therefore the more observant you are of your surroundings and the greater the detail you gather, the smoother and more comfortable your journey will be. Emotional Mapping and its component skills give you access to quality information (look at the difference between a city street guide and a detailed, geographical map) so that you are prepared for and can take advantage of your challenges and can recognize your successes.

Armed with all this understanding we are certain that you will feel inspired to explore other internal territories like your relationships with friends, family, religion, ambition, success and failure. On the way, remember to take time to consolidate and celebrate as you reach each milestone.

Bon voyage. We wish you well.

*Getting to know yourself is the beginning of a lifelong friendship.*

## A final word

Your experiences of Mapping are going to be very personal. Should you feel inclined, we would like to hear about them so please let us know how you get on. In order to take you further and to help you over any really difficult personal territory we are holding workshops and one-to-one facilitated sessions. If you want to help others overcome their obstacles we also offer Practitioner Training. You can contact us at A to Zen, PO Box 8856, London N10 3NB, UK, to receive further details.